The Golden Ages of Africa
John G. Jackson

The Golden Ages of Africa
John G. Jackson

American Atheist Press
Austin, TX
1987

American Atheist Press, P.O. Box 2117,
Austin, Texas, 78768-2117

© 1987 American Atheist Press. All rights reserved
Published February 1987.
Printed in the United States of America

ISBN 0-910309-36-1

ABOUT THE AUTHOR

John G. Jackson is an educator, lecturer, author, and man of principle. He was born on April 1, 1907, into a family of Methodists. As he remembers now, he has been an Atheist since he could think. The family minister once asked him when he was small, "Who made you?" After some thought, he replied from his own realization, "I don't know." He lived for fifty years in New York City, 1932 to 1977, lecturing at the "Ingersoll Forum" of the American Association for the Advancement of Atheism (from 1930 to 1955). During a parallel period he wrote articles for *The Truth Seeker* magazine. He was at the same time a writer and associate of the Rationalist Press Association in London, England, from 1932 to 1972.

Beginning in 1971, he became a lecturer in the Black Studies Department of Rutgers University, remaining there until 1973. From 1973 to 1977, he was a Visiting Professor at the University of New York. When he moved to Chicago, he quickly became a Visiting Professor at Northeast Illinois University, from 1977 to 1980. One of the courses which he taught was "Comparative Religion." His approach to that course was such that university officials cautioned him to "be more discreet." Another of his courses dealt with "Social Movements."

Jackson has been a consistent friend of labor and has been a member of the UAW, Dist. 65, AFL-CIO, for most of his life.

His books include *Introduction to African Civilizations; A Guide to the Study of African History, Ethiopia and the Origin of Civilization; Man, God and Civilization;* and best-selling *Pagan Origins of the Christ Myth* and *Christianity Before Christ.*

John G. Jackson

The first Golden Age of Africa began in prehistoric times, though there were several others in Ethopia, Egypt, North Africa, West Africa, and South Africa. Starting with the Pyramid Age of ancient Egypt around 6,000 years ago and continuing through the Golden Ages of West and East Africa, we encounter a time span of over 5,000 years. In round numbers we start our story about 4000 B.C. and conclude it at about A.D. 1600. Yet, a few years ago historical scholars wrote books on world history telling their readers that Africa had no history. The situation is a little better now, but a short discussion of the principal sources and authorities on the ancient and medieval history of Africa should be of value to serious students.

Professor Arnold J. Toynbee's *A Study of History* is considered a classic in the field of universal history. In the first volume of that work, the author tells us that the world up to now has produced twenty-one civilizations, and that all branches of humanity, except the Black race, have been creators of culture. In the words of Toynbee: "The Black race has not helped to create any civilization, while the Polynesian white race has helped to create one civilization, the brown race, two, the yellow race, three, the red race and the Nordic white race, four apiece, the Alpine white race, nine, and the Mediterranean white race, ten" (Arnold J. Toynbee. *A Study of History,* Vol. 1, p. 234. London: Oxford University Press, 1946). This statement by an eminent historian invites questioning, such as: "What about the ancient Egyptians?" That query would not have fazed Toynbee since he lists the Egyptians as members of the Mediterranean white race. Black scholars have tried to counter this false propaganda but with little success, for with the white racists controlling practically all the media of communication, the opposition has slight chance of reaching any kind of audience. Here, an example is in order. The late Professor William Leo Hansberry was a distinguished Africanist. While a student at Harvard, Hansberry was a pupil of Professor George A. Reisner, an eminent Egyptologist. One day when Reisner told his class that the ancient Egyptians were white people, Hansberry questioned the validity of that opinion. He mentioned the fact that the Greek historian, Herodotus, visited Egypt in the fifth century B.C. and described the people of that nation as being black skinned and curly haired. Of course the professor retorted by saying that he did not consider Herodotus to be an authority on that question. The student refused to be intimidated and reasonably replied that Herodotus was an eyewitness, and Reisner, thousands of years later, was not. Hansberry had hoped to study for a doctorate in Egyptology under Professor Reisner, but after the confrontation in class, this project never materialized. Finding the climate hostile at Harvard, young Hansberry went to Oxford University in England. He had no better luck there, and he never obtained his doctorate. After a lifetime of study, Professor Hansberry undertook to write a four-volume history of Africa. His untimely death occurred after the completion of two volumes of that work. To date none of this work has been published, and it does not seem likely it will be in the foreseeable future. When racists are confronted with the utter silliness of their propaganda, they never admit that they are wrong. They don't have to. When one controls the educational system, radio, television, the press, and practically all publishing houses, what chance does the opposition have? One of our friends, a very competent student of the City University of New York, was told by one of his professors that the ancient Egyptians were members of the white race. When the student cited Herodotus to the contrary, the professor told him that he did not consider the Father of History an authority. His reply was that "Herodotus was the Walter Winchell of the ancient world." Another example comes to mind: A distinguished Black scholar, a few years ago, visited the Metropolitan Museum of Art in New York City. He inquired of the young lady at the information desk as to the location of the African Collection. The young lady replied, "We don't have an African Collection." The professor then answered, "I meant to say the Egyptian Collection." Then the young lady said she could direct him to that collection, but opined, "We do not consider the Egyptians to be Africans or Egypt an African nation." The professor then opened up a map of Africa and invited the young lady to observe that Egypt was a part of Africa. "Wouldn't you say that Egypt was a part of Africa?" the scholar asked the young lady. Her answer was an indignant, "No!" Then the learned scholar replied, "Young lady, you are a jackass." The girl became hysterical and summoned the manager. When the African scholar showed his map of Africa to the manager and asked him if he would say that Egypt was a part of Africa, the reply was, "You could say so." The professor then asked, "Do you say so?" The reply was, "No, I do not." Then the Black scholar told him that he was also a jackass, and beat a hasty retreat, fearing that the management might summon the police.

We write about Africa and speak of Egypt as an African nation, but both of these names are of European origin. After the destruction of Carthage in the second century B.C., the Romans established a colony in North Africa and called it *Africa Romana*. The word *Africa* meant a place where the climate is hot. This word was probably derived from an Egyptian word *afr* which meant "fiery." When the Greeks were first admitted into Egypt in the seventh century B.C., they particularly admired the temple of *Ptah* in Memphis. So they called the country *Hekaptah* (the land of the temple of Ptah). Translated into Greek, this became *Aiguptos*. When the Romans conquered the Nile Valley, they Latinized *Aiguptos* into *Aegyptus* from whence we get *Egypt*. The ancient Egyptians called their country the land of *Ham, Kam,* or *Chem*. Literally, the word means *black,* referring to the rich black soil of the Nile Valley. They called themselves *Hamites,* or *Kamites,* or *Chemites*. From this word we get chemistry, since from this soil so many useful things were derived and changed in material form.

In studying African history we read of certain peoples being called Ethiopians, Hamites, Kushites, Moors, and Negroes. This calls for some discussion. In ancient times Africans in general were called *Ethiopians;* in medieval times most Africans were called *Moors*. In modern times some Africans were called *Negroes*. The Ethiopians were named by the Greeks. The name *Ethiopian* means "burnt face," from the Greek words *aithos* (burnt) plus *ops* (face or voice). This referred to the dark complexion of these Africans, which the Greeks attributed to sunburn brought on by their residence in the equatorial regions. In the literature on Africa, we are told that there are two groups of Africans, one progressive, the other, backward. The progressive peoples are called *Hamites, Kushites, Moors,* whereas the backward ones are called *Negroes*. The word *Negro* comes from *Niger,* a word of Latin derivation meaning "Black." Hamites, Kushites, and Moors were also Black, but they have been adopted into the white race. We are told that these people only appear to be black, since their dusky hue is only sunburn hiding their innate whiteness. The word *Negro* was manufactured during the slave trade.

There are many species of small fish in the ocean. When put into cans they are called *sardines*. There are no free fish called *sardines;* they only get that name when canned. Just so, no free Africans were called *Negroes;* they only got that name when enslaved. There is analogy here: Fish become sardines when imprisoned in cans, and Africans became Negroes when they were put in chains. According to American law, anybody with an African ancestry, however remote, is a Negro. Since the human race originated in Africa, then we all are Negroes. A word so vague as this does not mean anything at all. If the racists had to define their terms, they would soon go out of business. Since they do not have to do so, they are in for a long run of prosperity.

There is considerable literature on the ancient Ethiopians. If we follow the records, the original home of these people was in Africa, but the recognized authorities rarely concede this. Since there were also Ethiopians in Asia, they conclude that that was their earliest home and that they moved into Africa later on. At the present time the evidence seems to show Africa as the original seat of the Ethiopians, but we propose to examine the opinions of both schools of thought. From the writings of Homer and Herodotus we learn that the Ethiopians dwelt in the Sudan, Egypt, Arabia, Palestine, Western Asia, and India in days of old. This fact is mentioned by Sir Wallis Budge in his classic work on Ethiopian history:

> It seems certain that classical historians and geographers called the whole region from India to Egypt, both countries inclusive, by the name of Ethiopia, and in consequence they regarded all the dark skinned and black people who inhabited it as Ethiopians. Mention is made of Eastern and Western Ethiopians, and it is probable that the Easterners were Asiatics and the Westerners Africans (Sir E. A. Wallis Budge. *A History Of Ethiopia,* Vol. 1, p. VII. London: Metheun & Co., 1928).

According to Ephorus and Strabo the south coasts of both Africa and Asia were inhabited by Ethiopians. The traditions concerning King Memnon seem to show cultural connections between the two groups of Ethiopians. Herodotus credits King Memnon as the founder of Susa, the ancient capital of Elam, in Western Asia. The same Memnon was claimed as a king by the Ethiopians of the Upper Nile and was identified by the Egyptians with their pharaoh Amenhotep III. In the Old Testament book of Genesis we read that the sons of Ham were Kush, Mizraim, Phut, and Canaan, and that Kush begat Nimrod, and that the beginning of his kingdom was Babel and Erech and Kalneh in the land of Shinar (Mesopotamia). Here an ancient Babylonian kingdom is traced to a Kushite or Ethiopian origin and is culturally connected with Mizraim (Egypt), Phut (Libya), and Canaan (Palestine). From these traditions we may conclude that the earliest Babylonians were a branch of the Kushites or Ethiopians, connection by ties of kinship with the Egyptians, Canaanites, and the Libyans, but still more closely akin to the people who in ancient times dwelt on the banks of the Upper Nile. In the biblical tradition recorded in the tenth chapter of Genesis, the children of Ham spread out from Africa in two migrations — one through southern Arabia to Mesopotamia, and the other from Egypt through the land of Canaan into Syria. It seems highly probable that the people represented in Genesis by the legendary hero Nimrod, and among the Greeks by the eponym Belus, migrated from East Africa by way of Arabia to the Tigris-Euphrates Valley in times prior to recorded history. In 1854, a German scholar, Baron Bunsen, in the third volume of his *Philosophy of Universal History,* stated that Nimrod, the legendary father of the Babylonians, was in no way related to Kush (Ethiopia). It is true, said Bunsen, that these people of Mesopotamia had come from Africa, and so having come from the land of Kush, they were called Kushites, but the expression was purely geographical, for from a racial standpoint, they were akin to neither the Egyptians nor the Ethiopians. These sentiments of Baron Bunsen were refuted by the Orientalist, General Sir Henry Rawlinson, as follows:

> A laborious study of the primitive language of Chaldea led him [Sir Henry Rawlinson] to the conviction that the dominant race in Babylonia at the earliest time to which the monuments reached back was Kushite. He found the vocabulary of the primitive race to be decidedly Kushite, or Ethiopian, and he was able to interpret the inscriptions chiefly by the aid which was furnished to him from published works on the Galla (Abyssinian) and Mahra (South Arabian) dialects. He noted, moreover, a considerable resemblance in the system of writing which the primitive race employed, and that which was established from a very remote date in Egypt. Both were pictorial, both to a certain extent symbolic, both in some instances used identically the same symbols. Again, he found words in use among the Babylonians and their neighbors and kinsmen the Susianians, which seemed to be identical with ancient Egyptian or Ethiopian roots. The root *hyk* or *hak* which Manetho interprets as "king," and which is found in the well-known Hyksos, or Shepherd Kings, appeared in Babylonian and Susianian royal names under the form of *khak,* and as the terminal element, which is its position also in royal Ethiopic names. The name *Tirkak* is common to the royal lists of Susiana and Ethiopia, as that of Nimrod is to the royal names of Babylon and Egypt. The sun god is called *Ra* in Egyptian, and Ra was the Kushite name of the supreme god of the Babylonians. The author of Genesis unites together, as members of the same ethnic family, the Egyptians, the Ethiopians, the Southern Arabians, and the primitive inhabitants of Babylon. Modern ethnology finds, in the localities indicated, a number of languages, partly ancient, partly modern, which have common characteristics, and which evidently constitute one group. Egyptian, ancient and modern Ethiopian, as

represented by the Galla, Agau, etc., Southern Arabian (Himyaric and Mahra), and ancient Babylonian are discovered to be cognate tongues, varieties of one original form of speech (George Rawlinson. *The Origin of Nations,* pp. 212-214. New York: Scribner, Welford and Armstrong, 1878).

The people called primitive or Proto-Chaldeans by the brothers Rawlinson are now known as the Sumerians, the earliest civilized inhabitants of Mesopotamia. "This element," said Canon Rawlinson, "was predominantly Kushite. . . . In Susiana (Elam), where the Kushite blood was maintained in tolerable purity, there was, if we may trust the Assyrian remains, a very decided prevalency of a Negro type of countenance. The head was covered with short crisp curls, the eye was large, the nose and mouth nearly in the same line, the lips thick" (George Rawlinson. *The Five Great Monarchies of the Ancient Eastern World,* Vol. 2, p. 500. New York: Dodd, Mead & Co., 1870).

The best scholarship of both ancient and modern times has endorsed the Ethiopian theory of the origin of civilization, and now we can clearly see that this culture was of African origin. The advocates of Aryan and Semitic priority in ancient history have failed to sustain their case. A good statement in favor of Ethiopian priority was given by a Scottish anthropologist, who did research in the Orient for over thirty years. We refer to Major General J. G. R. Forlong, whom we are pleased to cite:

> It was undoubtedly Kushites who rendered possible the Aryan advance, and who played the part of a civilizing Rome, thousands of years before Roma's birth. It was their vast mythology and strange legends that passed, as Lord Bacon wrote, "like light air into the flutes of Grecians, there to be modulated as best suited Grecian fancies." Indeed it is manifest from many old writings, that it was their tales, myths, traditions, and histories that lay at the base of the Western world's thought and legendary lore. These so impressed all subsequent races, and entered so deeply and minutely into all Aryan mythologies, that many writers now think Aryans can only claim to have added to the superstructure and complexion of Ethiopian myths and mythical history, and let us remember that active Aryan life and mythologies began at least 3,000 years B.C., when high Asia . . . becoming too cramped for this race . . . was pressing southward to India and Ariana and to the west generally. Then and there must Aryans have met with Ethiopian civilization, as did Semites, when these began to group

themselves into nations about a thousand years later, or say, 2,000 B.C. They were all builders on old Kushite foundations (J. G. R. Forlong. *Rivers of Life,* Vol. 2, pp. 403-4. London: Bernard Quaritch, 1883).

From an exhaustive study of ancient history, a French scholar later arrived at similar conclusions. We let Professor Seignobos speak for himself:

> It is within the limits of Asia and Africa that the first civilized peoples had their development — the Egyptians in the Nile Valley, the Chaldeans in the plains of the Euphrates. They were people of sedentary and peaceful pursuits. Their skin was dark, the hair short and thick, the lips strong. Nobody knows their origin with exactness, and scholars are not agreed on the name to give them (some terming them Kushites, others Hamites). Later, between the twentieth and twenty-fifth centuries B.C., came bands of martial shepherds who had spread all over Europe and the west of Asia — the Aryans and the Semites (Charles Seignobos. *History of Ancient Civilization,* p. 17. London: T. Fisher Unwin, 1907).

Of the historical sources containing data on the Ethiopian origin of Egyptian civilization, the works of Herodotus and Diodorus are outstanding. *The History of Herodotus* was translated by George Rawlinson, with essays and notes by Sir Henry Rawlinson and Sir J. G. Wilkinson (four volumes) and published by Harper and Bros., New York and London, 1858. The same translation, edited by Manuel Komroff, was published in a one volume edition by Dial Press, New York, 1928, and reissued by Tudor Publishing Co., New York, 1939. The works of Diodorus Siculus have been published in the Loeb Classical Library in twelve volumes with Greek text and English translation by C. H. Oldfather. Volume 1 deals with the Egyptians and Volume 2 deals with the Ethiopians (London: William Heinemann Ltd. and Cambridge, Mass.: Harvard University Press. Vol. 1, 1933; Vol. 2, 1935). The historical authorities are mostly out of print and rare, but we will list them for the benefit of students who may find some of them in various libraries. Of great value and importance are: *The Ruins of Empires* by Count Volney published by Peter Eckler, New York, 1890. Another source by the same author is *New Researches in Ancient History,* J. P. Mendum, Boston, 1874. Another great work is *Anacalypsis,* 2 volumes, by Godfrey Higgins, published by Longmans, Green & Co., London,

1836. It was republished by The Macy-Masius Co., New York, 1927, and by University Books, New Hyde Park, N.Y. 1965. A scholarly study by an American was *Pre-historic Nations* by John D. Baldwin, Harper & Bros., New York 1869. Then there are the monumental six volumes of Gerald Massey: *A Book of the Beginnings*, 2 volumes, University Books, Secaucus, N.J., 1974; *The Natural Genesis*, 2 volumes, Samuel Weiser, Inc., New York, 1974; *Ancient Egypt: The Light of the World*, Weiser, New York, 1970. A German scholar, Professor Arnold Herman Ludwig Heeren, wrote *Historical Researches: African Nations* early in the nineteenth century. There is an English translation of the work, very rare, and out of print for over a hundred years. Fortunately the gist of this work was incorporated into *A Tropical Dependency* by Lady A. Lugard, Frank Cass & Co., London, 1964 and Barnes & Noble, New York, 1965. Lady Lugard was both a journalist and an historian, and her scholarship was impressive. Lady Lugard cited Heeren as follows:

> In Nubia and Ethiopia, stupendous, numerous and primeval monuments proclaim so loudly a civilization contemporary to, aye, earlier than that of Egypt, that it may be conjectured with the greatest confidence that the arts, sciences, and religion descended from Nubia to the lower country of Misraim; that civilization descended the Nile, built Memphis, and finally, sometime later, wrested, by colonization the Delta from the sea.

In commenting on the passage above, Lady Lugard wrote:

> The monuments though eloquent are not the only grounds upon which this conclusion has been reached. The fame of the Ethiopians was widespread in ancient history. Herodotus describes them as the tallest, the most beautiful and long-lived of the human race, and before Herodotus, Homer, in even more flattering language, described them as the most just of men — the favorites of the gods. The annals of all the great early nations of Asia Minor are full of them. The Mosaic records allude to them frequently, but while they are described as the most powerful, the most just, and the most beautiful of the human race, they are constantly spoken of as black, and there seems to be no other conclusion to be drawn, than that at that remote period of history, the leading race of the Western world was a black race. . . .
> The people of Ethiopia colonized to the north and west. Among their colonies to the north, one of the most important was Thebes.

Thebes and Meroe together founded the colony of Ammonium, in the western desert and through Thebes the religion of Meroe was carried into Lower Egypt. It was at a much later period, about 1500 B.C., that Egypt returned upon Meroe and conquered it. . . .

In corroboration of the view that the trade and influence of Meroe may have extended farther west than has yet been ascertained by modern exploration, I may mention a fact told me by Zebehr Pasha, when, . . . in 1886, he related to me the history of the foundation of his ephemeral empire in the Bahr-el-Ghazal. It was that, having occasion to act as the military ally of a certain native king, Tekkima, whose territory lay somewhere west and south of the spot marked upon modern maps as Dem Suleiman or Dem Zebehr — that is, presumably about 8°N and 25°E he was informed that he had to fight against magicians, who habitually came out of the earth, fought, and then disappeared. A careful system of scouting disclosed to him the fact that they came from underground, and when, after cutting off their retreat and conquering them, he insisted upon being shown their place of habitation, he found it to be deeply buried in the sand, a wonderful system of temples, "far finer," to use the words in which he described it, "than modern eyes have seen in the mosques of Cairo and Constantinople." It was, he said, such a work of massive stone as was done only by the great races of old. Through this underground city of stone, there ran a stream, and by the stream his native antagonists lived in common straw native huts. "Were your people, then," he asked them, "a nation of stone-cutters?" And they said, "Oh, no! This is not the work of our forefathers, but our forefathers found it here, and we have lived for many generations in these huts."

Whether this accidental discovery of unknown monuments may yet be repeated further west, and links be established in a continuous chain of ancient civilization reaching from the Red Sea to the country west of Chad, or whether the civilizations of the western and the eastern ends of the fertile belt of the Sudan were in fact separated from one another by a sea of which the waters of Chad are but the disappearing trace, is, however, a question which, interesting as it is, becomes in the light of the proved connection by the northern road, a question rather of detail rather than principle.

If there was no connection by the south, there certainly was connection by the north, by means of which the early inhabitants of the Hausa States may have been brought under the same influences of civilization which spread from Ethiopia to ancient Egypt and thence to Europe and North Africa (Lady A. Lugard. *A Tropical Dependency*. London: Frank Cass & Co., 1964 and New York: Barnes & Noble, 1965).

The first Golden Age of Egypt was inaugurated by an invasion from Ethiopia. In the words of Petrie:

> A conqueror of Sudani features founded the Third Dynasty and many entirely new ideas entered the country. This new movement culminated in the vast schemes of Khufu, one of history's most dominating personalities. With him the lines of Egyptian growth were established, and the course of events became the subject of the written record (Sir W. M. Flinders Petrie. *Modern Discovery of the Unknown Past* in the *Encyclopedia of Modern Knowledge*, p. 112. London: Amalgamated Press, 1936.)

The two most important structures of the Pyramid Age were the Great Pyramid and the Sphinx. The pyramid is said to have been built during the reign of Khufu, or Cheops. This would be between 4884 and 4854 B.C., according to MacNaughton (Duncan MacNaughton. *A Scheme of Egyptian Chronology*. London: Luzac Co., 1932). But MacNaughton claims that the building of this structure predated Khufu, and that it was actually commenced in the reign of King Zoser of the Third Dynasty, who reigned during the years 5345-5307 B.C. If this theory is correct, the building was originally an astronomical observatory, oriented to Sirius. According to MacNaughton:

> The first large stone building was the lower portion of what was later the Great Pyramid. As originally built, it was a flat-topped structure like the Babylonian Ziggurats. . . . Then came Khufu who conceived the idea of converting the old disused Sirius observatory into a pyramid tomb for himself, by continuing the slopes up to their present height, building in the King's Chamber in the process (ibid., 102-103).

The Sphinx, if we follow MacNaughton, was carved out of rock during the reign of Khafre (4726-4660 B.C.), a ruler of the Fifth Dynasty. But there is a tradition that the Sphinx was much older than the Great Pyramid. The French Egyptologist Pierre Hyppolyte Boussac gave it an estimated age of 10,000 years. An English scholar remarked that:

> In addition to the direct evidence for its prehistoric antiquity, it is certain that, if such a monument had been erected by any of the historic kings, it would have been inscribed with hieroglyphics, and the fact recorded in Manetho's lists and contemporary records, whereas all tradition of its origin seems to have been lost in the night of ages (Samuel Laing. *Human Origins*, p. 20. London: Watts & Co., 1913).

According to an inscription by King Khufu, the Sphinx was already ancient in his time. This fact was referred to by Massey, as follows:

> There is a stone in the museum at Boulak consecrated to the memory of a noteworthy transaction. We learn from it that in the time of Khufu, of the fourth dynasty, and founder of the Great Pyramid, that the Sphinx and its recently discovered temple, not only existed already, but were then in a state of dilapidation, and it is recorded in the inscription that he restored them (Gerald Massey, *A Book of the Beginnings*, Vol. 1, pp. 9-10. Secaucus, N.J.: University Books, 1974.)

A study of the Sphinx and the Great Pyramid by several modern scholars has revealed to us the great scientific knowledge possessed by the Egyptians six thousand years ago. There is much literature on this topic, but there is a recent book that is by far the best. We refer to *Secrets of the Great Pyramid* by Peter Tompkins, with an appendix by Livio Catullo Stecchini (New York: Harper & Row, 1971). The French astronomer and geodesist, Gian Domenico Cassini, suggested the establishment of a geodetic foot to facilitate accurate earth measurements in the seventeenth century, but he had been anticipated by Egyptian scientists of the Pyramid Age. In the words of Tompkins:

> Cassini, who very sensibly proposed the adoption of a geodetic foot representing 1/6000th part of a terrestrial minute of arc, would have been astounded had he known that just such a foot had been in existence for several millenia, and that the Sphinx, which could be used as a geodetic marker to indicate the equinox, also once had an obelisk between its paws, whose shadow could be used to compute not only the correct circumference of the earth, but the variance in the degree of latitude (Peter Tompkins.

Secrets of the Great Pyramid, p. 33. New York: Harper & Row, 1971).

A French astronomer, the Abbé Theophile Moreaux, some years ago wrote a book, *The Mysterious Science of the Pharaohs*. In that work he argued that the Great Pyramid was a scientific research institution. There were stored scientific instruments and calculations of standard weights and measures. In the King's Chamber was a granite slab, measuring one ten-millionth of the distance from either pole to the center of the earth. This distance, 3,949.79 miles, enables us to calculate the circumference of the earth as a great circle passing through the poles of 24,817.32 miles. Moreaux was convinced that the Egyptian astronomers knew this at least 6,000 years ago. The evidence presented by Tompkins and Stecchini in the book cited above has proven the Abbé Moreux was correct in his deductions. Stecchini refers to a papyrus of *The Book of the Dead* dating back to the First Dynasty. In chapter 64 of this document are data concerning the size and shape of the earth. We are told that the spirits of the netherworld are 4,601,200 in number, each twelve cubits high. The figure twelve suggests that the cubits are geographic measurements. Calculations are as follows:

12 x 4,601,200 cubits = 55,214,000 cubits = 138,036 geographic stadia, and this equals 2 diameters of the earth — polar and equatorial. Reducing these measurements to meters, we get the equatorial radius as 6,378,388 meters and the polar radius as 6,356,966 meters. From these figures the flattening of the North Pole may be calculated as 116/34,538, or 1/297.74. As Professor Stecchini points out:

> With extreme economy of numerical expression the Egyptians had arrived at values which are as good as the best modern ones. The figure for the equatorial radius happens to coincide to the meter with that calculated by Hayford. But Hayford calculated the polar flattening as 1/297. Halmert, however, set the polar flattening at 1/298.3, a figure which has been adopted in several of the recent surveys and calculations of the size of the earth which aim at achieving the maximum possible exactness (ibid., pp. 369-370).

Ordinarily we would not think of a deck of playing cards having any connection with the Great Pyramid. Peter Tompkins refers to a book by John B. Schmaltz, *Nuggets from King Solomon's Mines*, and remarks that:

Schmaltz demonstrated that the modern deck of cards could be taken as a symbol of the Egyptian year incorporated in the Great Pyramid. According to Schmaltz the 52 cards represent the weeks, the 12 face cards the months, the 13 cards in a suit the lunations, the suits, the seasons, the total face value of the cards (counting Jack as 11, Queen as 12 and King as 13), 364 days, plus the Joker as the magic 1.234, for a total of 365.234 days in the year (ibid., p. 112).

Among the secrets of the Great Pyramid were mathematical constants supposedly discovered in relatively modern times such as π (PI = 3.1416), ϵ (EPSILON = 2.71828), and ϕ (PHI = 1.618). To cite Tompkins again:

> Whoever built the Great Pyramid knew the dimensions of this planet as they were not to be known again until the seventeenth century of our era. They could measure the day, the year, and the Great Year of the Precession. They knew how to compute latitude and longitude very accurately by means of obelisks and the transits of stars. They knew the varying lengths of a degree of latitude and longitude at different locations on the planet and could make excellent maps, projecting them with a minimum of distortion. They worked out a sophisticated system of measures based on the earth's rotation on its axis which produced the admirably earth-commensurate foot and cubit which they incorporated in the Pyramid. In mathematics they were advanced enough to have discovered the Fibonacci series, and functions of π and ϕ (ibid., p. 285).

A lot of this ancient knowledge was hidden in the lost language of symbols. For instance, two black doves from Egypt were said to have founded the oracles of Dodona and Delphi in Greece. Herodotus noted that the doves were women and were pictured as black because they were Egyptians. A discussion in the appendix to the book cited above by Stecchini is pertinent:

> Delphi was considered the geodetic center of Greece. The god of Delphi, Apollo, whose name means the stone, was identified with an object, the *Omphalos* (navel), which has been found. It consisted of an ovoidal stone (the ovoidal shape indicated the lengthening of the degrees of latitude as one moves north) covered by a

net. The net was the symbol of what even today we call the net of meridians and parallels. The omphalos of Delphi was similar to the object which represented the god Amon in Thebes, the navel of Egypt. In 1966 I presented to the annual meeting of the Archaeological Institute of America a paper in which I maintained that historical accounts, myths, and legends, and some monuments of Delphi, indicate that the oracle was established there by the pharaohs of the Ethiopian Dynasty. This is the reason why the Greeks portrayed Delphos, the eponymous hero of Delphi, as a Negro (ibid., p. 349).

The art of writing, paper, ink, the pen, the alphabet, and the calendar were gifts of the early Golden Age of Africa to the world. Our calendar could have originated nowhere else except the valley of the Nile. Primitive men told time by watching the circumpolar stars. Later the month was measured by the four phases of the moon, each a week in duration, thus making up the four weeks of the month. The year was established by the inundation of the Nile, after the heliacal rising of Sirius at midsummer. The eight polar gods and the four compass gods of the Egyptian pantheon were merged to create the twelve zodiacal gods. The apparent annual passage of the sun through the twelve signs of the zodiac produced a year of 365¼ days, the fractional day being taken care of by leap year, an extra day at four-year intervals. Our calendar was born in Egypt on July 19, 4236 B.C. (John G. Jackson. *Man, God and Civilization*, pp. 227-9. New Hyde Park, N Y: University Books, 1972). Most books on history, astronomy, and astrology trace the origin of the zodiac to Babylonia or Greece and state that this knowledge later came to Egypt. This hypothesis is demonstrably false. Count Volney in his famous *Ruins of Empires* gave priority to the Ethiopians and the Egyptians. Cyril Fagan, an authority on the history of astrology, made the following statement:

> The examination of any popular Greco-Roman star atlas will show that the four successive constellations, Capricorn, Aquarius, Pisces, and Aries, are represented as being amphibious, if not entirely aquatic in form. Capricorn appears as a horned goat complete with fish's tail. Aquarius is but the Greek variant for *Hapi*, the god of the Nile; at the foot of the chained Andromeda swim the tethered fish (Pisces) while below the reposing Ram lurks Cetus, the sea-monster. These four constellations rose acronychally during the summer months of the Egyptian Inunda-

tion, when the Nile overflowed its banks and turned the land into a sea. This is yet another pointer to the fact that it was the Egyptians who named the constellations, and not the Babylonians as is commonly supposed. The representations of the zodiacal and other constellations are but ideograms, differing but little from those which compose Egyptian hieroglyphic writings. In the unrolling papyrus of the eastern skies, the whole story of the Inundation can be read at dusk in the rising of these four constellations. Their symbolism fits only Egypt, for she alone of all the nations of antiquity suffered the annual transformation of her countryside into an immense lake, during the four months when these constellations rose at eve (Cyril Fagan. *Astrological Origins,* p. 126. St. Paul, Minnesota: Llewellyn Publications, 1973).

The glories of the Pyramid Age ended at the death of King Neterkere in 4163 B.C. He was the last ruler of the Sixth Dynasty. Regression and chaos prevailed from the Seventh Dynasty through the Tenth Dynasty (4163-3554 B.C.). The period of decline was ended by Intef, founder of the Eleventh Dynasty, and the first ruler of the Middle Kingdom. The next king was Intef II, who was followed by five Mentuhoteps. After these Amenemhet I established the Twelfth Dynasty. This monarch was a man of uncommon ability. The reign of Sesostris I (3373-3327 B.C.) featured imperial expansion, and the boundaries of Egypt were extended southward to the Kingdom of Kush. Amenemhet II led armies into Sinai, and Sesostris III extended the conquest into Syria. In 3184 B.C., Amenemhet IV died, leaving no heir to the throne. In Egypt, as in most other African nations, the succession was inherited through the female line, that is, through the daughter of the ruler. The new queen passed on the regal power to her husband, who became the next king. The kingly office passed from father to son-in-law. It was the custom to have the oldest son of the king marry his oldest sister through whom the royal prerogatives were transmitted. This made the king's son likewise his son-in-law and preserved his right of succession to the throne. In conformity with custom, Amenemhat IV had married his sister, Sebeknefrure. Since this ruler had died childless, the queen was privileged to select the next pharaoh, since, by law, her husband would inherit the crown. Queen Sebeknefrure was expected to marry a Theban nobleman and elevate him to the throne. Instead, she chose, as a husband, a commoner of Lower Egypt. Since the Theban nobility refused to accept a northerner from the Delta as their sovereign, a civil war ensued, and it lasted for nearly a century. While this unnecessary strife was going on, the Hyksos, or Shepherd Kings, invaded the country from a base in Asia, conquering first the Delta and then moving up the river to Thebes. The Hyksos were dominant during the Fifteenth, Sixteenth, and Seventeenth Dynasties, a period of about 150 years. While the country was under foreign dominion, certain Theban nobles traveled south to Kush and organized an underground liberation movement. The Hyksos were expelled from Thebes by an army led by King Sekenenre. Ahmose I, who ascended the throne in 1709 B.C., led his army northward, liberated Memphis and drove the Shepherd Kings out of Egypt and into the desert of Sinai. This was the beginning of the Eighteenth Dynasty and of the New Kingdom. The new line of rulers erected palaces and temples at Thebes which were among the wonders of the world. Under Thutmose I (1662-1628 B.C.), Egyptian imperialism reached its zenith. This phase of Egyptian history has been admirably summarized by Professor James Henry Breasted (James Henry Breasted. *Cambridge Ancient History,* Vol. 2, p. 88. London: University Press, 1926).

The true glory of the age culminated in the reign of Amenhotep III (1538-1501 B.C.). Timber was imported from Syria, and large seaworthy ships were constructed. With this fleet the mariners and merchants of Egypt sailed along the East African coast and traded with the people of Punt, from whom they imported cargoes of gold, ivory, spices, ebony, and ostrich feathers. The domain of Amenhotep III extended from the confines of Kush to the plains of Shinar. The city of Thebes expanded into a mighty metropolis with walls nine miles in circumference. In the suburbs, splendid mansions were erected for the nobility, some of them containing fifty or sixty rooms. On their walls were fine paintings. These homes were fitted out with costly and attractive inlaid furniture and adorned with beautiful vases and skillfully carved ornaments and utensils of bronze, ivory, and ebony. Superb temples were built on the riverfront, by order of the king, and were linked together by impressive avenues of sphinxes. Around the mansions and temples were tree-lined boulevards and gardens of flowers with the adjacent landscape enhanced by a series of lakes. As the horse had been introduced into Egypt by the Hyksos, the system of transportation was improved. Bigger and better roads were built, and Egyptian gentlemen traversed the highways in swift horse-drawn chariots.

The Nineteenth Dynasty began with the reign of Hormhab (1454-1395 B.C.), but the great ruler of this dynasty was Rameses II (1394-1328 B.C.). In a reign of sixty-six years this monarch conquered extensive territories in Western Asia and built colossal temples in the Nile Valley. Six of these temples were erected in Ethiopia and dedicated to Amon,

Ra, and Ptah. The king and queen were also accorded divine status and appropriately worshipped. In referring to the six temples, Breasted stated that:

> In all of them, Rameses was more or less prominently worshipped, and in one, his queen, Nefertiti, was the presiding divinity. Of his Nubian sanctuaries, The Great Rock Temple at Abu Simbel is the finest, and deservedly the goal of modern travellers in Egypt (James Henry Breasted. *A History of Egypt*, pp. 374-5. New York: Bantam Books, 1967).

Rameses III (1230-1199 B.C.) of the Twentieth Dynasty was also a great ruler. He was succeeded by eight kings, all bearing the name of Rameses, but none of these became great. After a decline of several centuries, Egypt's greatness was restored by an Ethiopian invasion in 761 B.C. led by King Piankhi of Kush. During the decade of 761-751, this monarch ruled over both Ethiopia and Egypt. The Kushite king from his palace in Napata objected to the tribute of gold, cattle, and soldiers which he was required to deliver to King Osorkon III of Egypt. So fitting out a fleet and recruiting an army, he besieged Hermopolis. The local ruler, King Namlot, surrendered the city to the Ethiopian conqueror. From an inscription of Piankhi we learn that:

> Hermopolis threw herself upon her belly and pleaded before the king. Messengers came forth, and descended, bearing everything beautiful to behold: gold, every splendid costly stone, clothing in a chest, and the diadem which was upon his head, the uraeus, which inspireth fear of him without ceasing during many days.

On visiting the royal stables, Piankhi was shocked by the malnutrition among the horses, a result of the siege of the city. So he said to the former ruler: "By God! I swear it grieves me more that these horses have been starved than any other mischief that you, Namlot, have caused." At another city, farther down the Nile, the Ethiopian conqueror delivered an ultimatum:

> You suicidal, silly, and miserable creatures! If an hour passes without you opening your gates to me, you are dead men, and as it would be painful of me to have to kill you, do not close the door on life, and do not court death in this manner!

The garrison of the city capitulated and not one life was lost. At the approach to another city the order given was: "Open your gates and you shall live; close them, and you shall die." Again, the garrison surrendered, and Piankhi entered the city and held a service of thanksgiving in the local temple. Continuing down the river he next took Memphis, and eventually Heliopolis, where King Osorkon III of Bubastis yielded his regal powers to the Ethiopian potentate. On returning to Napata, Piankhi had a granite stela erected in the Temple of Amen, and on the four sides of the monument, he described his successful campaign in detail. This record possesses intrinsic merit, and has been appraised by Professor Breasted as follows:

> It displays literary skill and an appreciation of dramatic situations which is notable, while the vivacious touches found here and there quite relieve it of the arid tone usual in such hieroglyphic documents. The imagination endues the personages appearing here more easily with life than those of any other similar historical narrative of Egypt; and the humane Piankhi especially, the lover of horses, remains a *man* far removed from the conventional companion and equal of the gods, who inevitably occupied the exalted throne of the pharaohs in all other such records (James Henry Breasted. *A History of Egypt,* p. 456. New York: Bantam Books, 1967).

Piankhi was the outstanding ruler of the Twentieth Dynasty. He was followed by King So (751-720 B.C.), the last ruler of the Twenty-Third Dynasty. The Twenty-fourth Dynasty consisted of one monarch, King Bocchoris, who, according to Manetho, reigned only six years (720-714 B.C.). The Twenty-fifth Dynasty has been called the Kushite or Ethiopian Dynasty, which began in 714 B.C., when, as Herodotus related: "Egypt was invaded by a vast army of Ethiopians, led by Sabacos, their king" (*The History of Herodotus,* translated by George Rawlinson, p. 129. New York: Tudor Publishing Co., 1939). This ruler, better known as Shabaka (714-702 B.C.), conquered Lower Egypt and there established Ethiopian supremacy. An invasion of Western Asia followed, where Shabaka's army escaped defeat only by an outbreak of plague among the soldiers of the Assyrians. The next sovereign, Shabataka (702-690 B.C.), was slain by Taharka, who seized the crown and established his capital at Tanis. The reign of this pharaoh was noted for its prosperity and cultural advance. The Egyptologist Sir Arthur Weigall has referred to this period of Egyptian history as: "That astonishing epoch of Nigger dominion" (Sir Arthur Weigall. *Flights into Antiquity*, p. 222. London: Hutchinson & Co., 1928).

The last great African monarch to rule over Egypt was Ahmose II (569-525 B.C.) of Libyan ancestry. Known to the Greeks as Amasis, he was a great statesman but failed to save Egypt from foreign domination. The best soldiers of the Egyptian armies had years before left the country and pledged their allegiance to the Ethiopian king at Meroe. So Amasis had to rely on Libyan and Greek mercenaries for defense against alien invasion. Being an able diplomat, he kept Egypt free until his death early in 525 B.C. His successor, Psamtik III, was overthrown by a Persian invasion after a rule of only six months. This was the beginning of the Twenty-seventh Dynasty. Four puppet dynasties under Persian control lasted until 332 B.C., when the Greeks under Alexander the Great became the new masters of Egypt. The Alexandrian Age was continued under the Ptolemies until 30 B.C., when Egypt became a Roman province under the rule of the Caesars. From Menes to Amasis spanned a period of nearly five thousand years. The achievements of this great African nation under its native rulers was indubitably praiseworthy. A good short summary was penned by a contemporary German scholar:

> The insurgent Amasis stood at the end of Egypt's history, but at its beginning lay the Nile mud, which came from the interior of Africa. ... Egypt was a great kingdom created by Africans. ... Of African inspiration are the pyramids, the golden burial chambers, the statues, plastic arts, temple friezes, and other great Egyptian works of art. The Sphinx is an African monument, the hieroglyphs are an African script, and Ammon, Isis, and Osiris are African gods. So great was the achievement of the Africans in the Nile Valley that all the great men of ancient Europe journeyed there — the philosophers Thales and Anaximander, the mathematician Pythagoras, the statesman Solon, and an endless stream of historians and geographers, whose works are all based on Herodotus' outstanding description of Egypt, to which the second volume of his history entirely was devoted (Herbert Wendt. *It Began in Babylon: The Story of the Birth and Development of Races and Peoples*, p. 58. Boston: Houghton Mifflin Co., 1962).

Another contributor to the Golden Ages of Africa was the city-state of Carthage in North Africa. This city, one of the great cultural centers of antiquity, was destroyed by the Romans after the final defeat of the

Carthaginians at the end of the Third Punic War. The Carthaginians, like their other Phoenician brothers, were great merchants and mariners. They practiced peaceful pursuits and neglected military matters, and this led to their ultimate defeat at the hands of the Romans. After losing Sicily to the Romans in 242 B.C., the Carthaginians were confronted with a rebellion of their Libyan vassals, and in order to prevent Roman aid to the rebels, they were compelled to surrender the island of Sardinia to the Romans. The Second Punic War was waged in Europe and Africa with Hannibal leading the Carthaginians and Cornelius Scipio commanding the Roman forces. A series of blunders on the part of Hannibal brought defeat to the Carthaginians at the battle of Zama in 202 B.C. The Roman peace terms were harsh, for over a period of fifty years, Carthage was compelled to pay an indemnity of about $20,000,000. All Carthaginian military power was confiscated by the Romans, and the founding of new colonies or involvement in foreign wars was forbidden, unless approved by Rome. The great African city-state might have survived all these disabilities, but in 150 B.C. King Massanissa of Numidia, an African ally of Rome, invaded Carthaginian territory. The Carthaginians counterattacked in self-defense, and this led to the Third Punic War. This war, begun by Rome in 149 B.C. under the trumped-up charge that a treaty had been violated, raged for three years. In 146 B.C. the city of Carthage was captured by the Romans and completely destroyed by fire. In the words of Professor Hapgood:

> They burned the great city of Carthage, their ancient enemy, and their incalculable superior in everything relating to science. The library of Carthage is said to have contained about 500,000 volumes, and these, no doubt, dealt with the history and sciences of Phoenicia as a whole (Charles H. Hapgood. *Maps of the Ancient Sea Kings*, p. 196. New York & Philadelphia: Chilton Book Co., 1960).

The Golden Age in Africa continued to flourish for three centuries under the Alexandrine Ptolemies. Alexander the Great had planned to build a new city on the Mediterranean coast of Egypt shortly before his untimely death. The city was actually constructed by Alexander's successor, Ptolemy I, who appropriately named the new city Alexandria. This city was built on a strip of land about six miles long and two miles wide between the Mediterranean Sea and Lake Mareotis. In the harbor of Alexandria was the island of Pharos on which was erected a lighthouse built of marble with a pinnacle souring four hundred feet upward.

In its summit shone a light visible thirty miles out at sea. The walls of the city were about fifteen miles in circumference, and the layout of the city was quite modern with streets running north-south and east-west and intercrossing at right angles. Canopie Street traversed the metropolis in an east-west direction for five or six miles. Over one hundred feet wide, it was lined on both sides by marble colonnades. Another boulevard, equally elegant, ran in the north-south direction. These avenues were lined with attractive palms and illuminated with lamps at night. The palaces, mansions, and public buildings were faced with white marble and polished granite. By day the glare of the sun was moderated by utilizing veils and curtains of green silk. The tomb of Alexander the Great was located at the intersection of the two main thoroughfares of the city. This mausoleum was surrounded by gardens, fountains, and obelisks. The glory of Alexandria was the museum commenced by Ptolemy I (Soter), and completed by his son Ptolemy II (Philadelphus). The outstanding feature of the museum located in the Bruchion (the aristrocratic quarter of the city) and adjoining the Royal Palace was the Philadelphian Library. Surrounding its collection of about 400,000 books were the finest pictures and statues of the age. Another library was established in the Serapeum (The Temple of Serapis), and this collection contained about 300,000 volumes. In the establishment of the museum (actually a university) and its libraries, Ptolemy Soter had in mind three goals: (1) The preservation of extant knowledge, (2) The acquisition of new knowledge, and (3) The diffusion of knowledge.

Callimachus, the first chief librarian, undertook a collection of the sacred books of the Ethiopians, Elamites, Persians, Indians, Babylonians, Assyrians, Phoenicians, Syrians, and Greeks. The chief librarian was commissioned by royal command to purchase whatever books that were available at the expense of the government. All books brought into Egypt by foreigners were appropriated by the library, where correct copies were transcribed. A copy was returned to the owner, and the original was retained by the library. These acquisitions were well paid for. Ptolemy III (Euergetes) bought from a citizen of Athens certain works of Aeschylus, Euripides, and Sophocles. Transcripts of these works were returned to the owner, plus an indemnity of about $15,000. The museum has sometimes been called the University of Alexandria, for it contained faculties of mathematics, astronomy, medicine, and literature. Connected with the museum were geological and botanical gardens, a chemical laboratory, an astronomical observatory, and an anatomical dissection room. The scientists and scholars of the establishment were especially celebrated in the fields of mathematics, astronomy, and geography. The most famous of the Alexandrian savants was Euclid, the author of a book on geometry, that was used as a textbook in the schools of the world for over two thousand years. Another mathematician of the same school was Apollonius, who wrote treatises on the sonic sections. Also on the staff of the museum was Archimedes, a mathematician, physicist, and engineer. Among the astronomers were Eratosthenes, Claudius Ptolemy, Hipparchus, and Sosigines. Among the engineers and inventors were Ctesibius, inventor of the single cylinder fire engine, and his pupil, Hero, who gave the engine two cylinders. Hero also invented a steam engine, a forerunner of the modern steam turbine. As a scientific research center the museum flourished for about a hundred years, then went into a decline. The Philadelphian Library was destroyed by fire in 48 B.C., when a Roman army led by Julius Caesar captured Alexandria. The Serapian Library was destroyed in A.D. 389 by a fanatical mob of Christian monks. After the end of the Alexandrian Age, the Romans became the new custodians of civilization. This was unfortunate, for the Romans lacked the intellectual receptivity of the Greeks. Mentally, the Greeks were eggheads (highbrows) and the Romans were jug heads (lowbrows).

The racists argue that Europe gave civilization to Africa. This is a complete inversion of the truth. The first civilized Europeans were the Greeks, and it is a matter of record that they were civilized by the Africans of ancient Egypt. The Greeks passed on this culture to the Romans, who finally lost it, bringing a 500 year period of decline known as the Dark Ages. Civilization was restored to Europe by another group of Africans, the Moors, who brought the Dark Ages to an end and thus re-civilized the barbarians of Europe. During the Golden Age of Islam, the Empire of the Two Shores, with branches in Africa and Europe, was the most advanced state in the world from a cultural viewpoint. A short survey of this brilliant era of human culture would be of value to the student, but we do not have the space for it. We advise the reader to consult such authorities as Winwood Reade's *The Martyrdom of Man,* Stanley Lane-Poole's *The Story of the Moors in Spain,* and Lady Lugard's *A Tropical Dependency.* To cite the last named:

> Throughout the dark period of the Middle Ages when the [Roman] Catholic Church was asserting its claim to dominate the conscience of the western world, . . . all that was independent, all that was progressive, all that was persecuted for conscience's sake, took refuge in the courts of Africa. Art, science, poetry, and

wit found congenial homes in the orange-shaded arcades of the College of Fez, in the palaces of Morocco, and in the exquisite gardens of Tripoli and Tunis (Lady A. Lugard. *A Tropical Dependency*, p. 73 London: Frank Cass & Co., 1964 and New York: Barnes & Noble, 1965).

The Golden Age in West Africa lasted from ancient times until the sixteenth century of the Christian Era. The great states of this period were Ghana, Mali, Songhay, Kanem, Bornu, and the Hausa States. In the medieval period, from about the tenth to the sixteenth century, the African Golden Age flourished among the Swahilis in the trading cities of the East African coast. Information on these topics may be obtained from chapters 5 and 7 of *Introduction to African Civilizations*, by John G. Jackson. In that work the reader will find references to sources and authorities for further study. In the recent past we have told students about the scholars of Timbuktu in the sixteenth century, and were invariably asked was not Timbuktu a mythical place akin to the lost Atlantis? The students were assured that Timbuktu the Mysterious was a great city five hundred years ago and were given some details of its history. Again we have to thank Lady Lugard for preserving some of the lost pages of African history.

The University of Sankore in Timbuktu enjoyed considerable prestige as a seat of higher education during the reign of Askia the Great of the Songhay Empire. In the middle of the sixteenth century a large and learned society of literati flourished in Timbuktu. Professor Ahmed Baba, one of the greatest scholars of his time, has left us a sketch of one of the masters under whom he had studied in his youth. This distinguished professor, Mohammed Abu Bekr of Sankore, is said to have been "one of the best of God's virtuous creatures." Besides this:

> He was a working scholar, and a man instinct with goodness . . . Everyone who knew him loved him . . . He taught his pupils to love science, to follow its teachings, to devote their time to it, to associate with scholars, and to keep their minds in a state of docility. He lavishly lent his most precious books, rare copies, and the volumes that he most valued, and never asked for them again, no matter what was the subject of which they treated. . . . His intelligence was broad and luminous. His usual manner was taciturn and grave, but he would occasionally break into sallies of wit (ibid., pp. 204-6).

This highly civilized African culture was brought to an end by a Moorish invasion of the Songhay Empire in the latter part of the sixteenth century. The deplorable results have been described as follows:

> All that was cultivated, all that was enlightened, all that was rich, refined, and influential was driven out, and the greater number of men, women, and children were taken in chains across the desert. ... The sack of Timbuktu was the signal for the letting loose of all the evils of lawless tyranny upon the country. From this time the history of the Sudan becomes a mere record of riot, robbery, and decadence (ibid., pp. 309-310).

Al Masudi of Bagdad visited the East African coast in A.D. 912. In a famous book, *Meadows of Gold and Mines of Gems* (9 volumes in the French translation. There is a one volume English abridgment), this historian tells of what he saw and heard in his extensive travels. The people who lived on the African shores of the Indian Ocean were called the *Zanj,* that is to say, the Black people. The various groups of East Africans lived in a territory about 2,500 miles long from the Horn of Africa to Mozambique. The ships of the Arabs went as far south as Sofala. Masudi referred to a Kingdom of Waqlimi, which was probably located in what is now called Rhodesia. By the fourteenth century the Swahilis had built a number of prosperous trading cities on the East African coast. Among them were Malindi, Mombasa, Kilwa, and Zanzibar. In A.D. 1331, a famous Moorish traveller visited this region. He was particularly impressed with Kilwa. This visitor, Ibn Batuta, remarked that:

> Then I set off by sea from the town of Mogadishu for the land of the Swahili and the town of Kilwa, which is in the land of the Zanj. We arrived at Mombasa, a large island two days journey from the land of the Swahili. ... We spent a night on the island, and then set sail for Kilwa, the principal town on the coast the greater part of whose inhabitants are Zanj of very black complexion ... Kilwa is one of the most beautiful and well-constructed towns in the world. The whole of it is elegantly built (Ibn Batuta. *East African Coast: Select Documents,* p. 31. Oxford: The Clarendon Press, 1962).

Unfortunately the Portuguese sent their fleets and armies into this territory in the early sixteenth century and destroyed the Swahili trading ports. Thus, another phase of the Golden Ages of Africa was brought to an end. This period in history is discussed by Basil Davidson in *The Lost Cities of Africa*, and in *The African Past*. The Golden Ages of Africa had their ups and downs, but African culture has maintained a certain persistency of survival. This has been well expressed by a contemporary African scholar:

> Nubia appears to be closely akin to Egypt and the rest of Black Africa. It seems to be the starting point of both civilizations. So we are not astonished today to find many civilizing features common to Nubia, whose kingdom lasted until the British occupation, and the remainder of Black Africa. Right after the end of Egypto-Nubian Antiquity, the Empire of Ghana soured like a meteor from the mouth of the Niger to the Senegal River, circa the third century A.D. Viewed in this perspective, African history proceeded without interruption. The first Nubian dynasties were prolonged by the Egyptian dynasties until the occupation of Egypt by the Indo-Europeans, starting in the fifth century B.C. Nubia remained the sole source of culture and civilization until about the sixth century A.D., and then Ghana seized the torch from the sixth century until 1240, when its capital was destroyed by Sundiata Keita. This heralded the launching of the Mandingo Empire (capital Mali), of which Delafosse would write: "Nevertheless, this little village of the Upper Niger was for several years the principal capital of the largest empire ever known in Black Africa, and one of the most important ever to exist in the universe." Next came the Empire of Gao, the Empire of Katenga (or Mossi, still in existence), the kingdoms of Djoloff and Cayor (in Senegal) destroyed by Faidherbe under Napoleon III. In listing this chronology, we have simply wanted to show that there was no interruption in African history. It is evident that, if starting from Nubia and Egypt, we had followed a continental geographical direction, such as Nubia — Gulf of Benin, Nubia — Congo, Nubia — Mozambique, the course of African history would still have appeared to be uninterrupted (Cheikh Anta Diop. *The African Origin of Civilization*, pp. 147-8. New York & Westport: Lawrence Hill & Co., 1974).

Sometimes students ask how was it that Africa gave the world civilization and was in the forefront of social progress for thousands of years, and then retrogressed to the point where it (Africa) was taken out of history? So now we are striving to restore the lost pages of African history.

FURTHER READING

There is a great book that deals with the subject of African history: *The Destruction of Black Civilization* by Professor Chancellor Williams (Chicago: Third World Press, 1974).

OTHER BOOKS FROM AMERICAN ATHEIST PRESS

The Bible Handbook by G.W. Foote & W.P. Ball _____ $7.00
Everything is here: absurdities, indecencies, contradictions, unfulfilled prophecies, broken promises of god, obscenities, sado-masochisms, impossibilities. Paperback. 400 pp. (5008)

All the Questions You Ever Wanted to Ask American Atheists — with All the Answers by Madalyn O'Hair & Jon G. Murray _____ $8.00
The experience of 20 years of Atheist work is distilled into this 359-page paperback. (5356)

Pagan Origins of the Christ Myth by John G. Jackson _____ $3.00
This is one of the American Atheist Press' best-selling books. No wonder, since it takes on the question most historians of the Roman empire era have not had the guts to ask — did Christ exist? The answer is NO! Find out why. Paperback. 30 pp. (5204)

American Atheist Heritage by Joseph Lewis _____ $4.00
Abraham Lincoln, Benjamin Franklin, Thomas Jefferson, and Luther Burbank nowadays are described as religious men. This is a preposterous claim. They were too intelligent to be fools. Here are the facts. Paperback. 54 pp. (5212)

Women and Atheism: The Ultimate Liberation by Madalyn O'Hair _____ $2.50
This is the unexpurgated chapter of *Freedom Under Siege*, which was seriously censored in that publication. The full story of Christianity's oppression, suppression and repression of women. Paperback. 22 pp. (5420)

The Case Against Religion by Dr. Albert Ellis _____ $4.00
Religion is a mental illness — and this famous psychiatrist proves it! Paperback. 57 pp. (5096)

Why I Am an Atheist by Madalyn O'Hair _____ $3.25
Basic American Atheism combined with a history of Materialism, upon which Atheism is predicated. Paperback. 39 pp. (5416)

Why I Left the Roman Catholic Church by Charles Davis _____ $3.00
A damning condemnation by the man who had risen to head the Roman Catholic Church in England, then quit in disgust. Learn why. Paperback. 27 pp. (5080)

Atheist Primer by Madalyn O'Hair _____ $3.00
Gods are figments of human imagination. This fact is clearly and humorously explained in simple language a small child can easily understand. Illustrated children's book. Paperback. 30 pp. (5372)

A Few Reasons for Doubting the Inspiration of the Bible by Robert G. Ingersoll _____ $3.00
The great 19th-century Atheist presents 61 compelling arguments as to the absurdity of the Bible, or that its source was an alleged god. Paperback. 30 pp. (5152)

(Texas Residents please add 6¼% sales tax.)

Order from:
American Atheist Press, P.O. Box 2117, Austin, TX 78768-2117

The *American Atheist* Magazine

This is where it will happen; in this journal, the new intellectuals, American Atheists, will hammer out the philosophy of living and the moral/ethical values of our nation — for now and for the future.

This is *the* journal of Atheist news and thought! It is dedicated in spirit and content to Atheist activism — *doing* something about the drive organized religion is making to turn the United States into a theocracy, rather than debating the issue with philosophical detachment. Its purpose is educational: to inform Atheists about the doings of Atheist activists in the U.S.A. and all the world, and to provide the knowledge which *proves* the Atheist position that Atheism is the only viable life-style, both intellectual and social, in a civilization that has advanced to the point where robot probes explore the planets and the awesome secrets of DNA are being unlocked.

This magazine contains cartoons for which the editors are constantly reprimanded, "blasphemous" articles concerned with the most holy of holies, exposés of religious monetary shenanigans, private peeks into the marriage of politicians lusting for power and churches out for tax dollars, historical articles on great American Atheists, investigations into religious frauds, poetry, book reviews, an exciting "Letters to the Editor" section, and regularly-featured columnists offering opinions on nearly everything.

Though a subscription to the *American Atheist* is free to members of American Atheists, it is also available to non-members on a yearly subscription basis.

☐ Subscription, $25/year
☐ Foreign subscription, $35/year
☐ Sustaining subscription, $50/year
   (tax-deductable)
☐ Sample copy, $2

Last name: _____ First name: _____
Address: _____
City/State/Zip: _____

☐ I am enclosing a check or money order for $ _____ payable to American Atheists.
☐ Please charge my credit card for $ _____ . ☐ Visa or ☐ Mastercard

Return to:
American Atheists
P.O. Box 2117
Austin, TX 78768-2117

"AIMS AND PURPOSES"
(as recorded in documents of incorporation)
AMERICAN ATHEISTS ARE ORGANIZED:

(1) to stimulate and promote freedom of thought and inquiry concerning religious beliefs, creeds, dogmas, tenets, rituals, and practices;

(2) to collect and disseminate information, data, and literature on all religions and promote a more thorough understanding of them, their origins, and their histories;

(3) to advocate, labor for, and promote in all lawful ways the complete and absolute separation of state and church;

(4) to advocate, labor for, and promote in all lawful ways the establishment and maintenance of a thoroughly secular system of education available to all;

(5) to encourage the development and public acceptance of a humane ethical system, stressing the mutual sympathy, understanding, and interdependence of all people and the corresponding responsibility of each individual in relation to society;

(6) to develop and propagate a social philosophy in which man is the central figure, who alone must be the source of strength, progress, and ideals for the well-being and happiness of humanity;

(7) to promote the study of the arts and sciences and of all problems affecting the maintenance, perpetuation, and enrichment of human (and other) life; and

(8) to engage in such social, educational, legal, and cultural activity as will be useful and beneficial to members of American Atheists and to society as a whole.

"DEFINITIONS"

Atheism is the *Weltanschauung* (comprehensive conception of the world and of total human life value systems) of persons who are *free* from theism — i.e., *free from* religion. It is predicated on ancient Greek Materialism.

American Atheism may be defined as the mental attitude that unreservedly accepts the supremacy of reason and aims at establishing a life-style and ethical outlook verifiable by experience and the scientific method, independent of all arbitrary assumptions of authority or creeds.

Materialism declares that the cosmos is devoid of immanent conscious purpose; that it is governed by its own inherent, immutable, and impersonal laws; that there is no supernatural interference in human life; that man — finding his resources within himself — can and must create his own destiny. Materialism restores to man his dignity and his intellectual integrity. It teaches that we must prize our life on earth and strive always to improve it. It holds that man is capable of creating a social system based on reason and justice. Materialism's "faith" is in man and man's ability to transform the world culture by his own efforts. This is a commitment which is in every essence life-asserting. It considers the struggle for progress as a moral obligation and impossible without noble ideas that inspire man to struggle and bold creative works. Materialism holds that humankind's potential for good and for an outreach to more fulfilling cultural development is, for all practical purposes, unlimited.

American Atheists is a non-political, non-profit, educational organization. Another of its functions is to act as a "watchdog" to challenge any attempted breach of what Thomas Jefferson called "the wall of separation between state and church," upon which principle our nation was founded.

Membership is open only to those who are in accord with the "Aims and Purposes" above indicated and who are Atheist Materialists. Membership in the national organization is a prerequisite for membership in state, county, city, or local chapters. Membership fee categories are reflected on the reverse side of this sheet (American Atheists Membership Application form).

A complete copy of the Constitution and By-Laws of American Atheists is available upon request. Send $1.00 for postage and handling to:

Constitution and By-Laws
American Atheists
P.O. Box 2117
Austin, TX 78768-2117

Membership Application For American Atheists

Last name: _____ First name: _____
  Companion's name (if family or couple membership)
Last name: _____ First name: _____
Address: _____
City/State/Zip: _____

  This is to certify that I/we am/are in agreement with the "Aims and Purposes"* and the "Definitions"* of American Atheists. I/we consider myself/ourselves to be Materialist or Non-theist (*i.e.*, A-theist) and I/we have, therefore, a particular interest in the separation of state and church and American Atheists' efforts on behalf of that principle.

  I/we usually identify myself/ourselves for public purposes as (check one):
  ☐ Atheist   ☐ Objectivist   ☐ Agnostic
  ☐ Freethinker   ☐ Ethical Culturalist ☐ Realist
  ☐ Humanist   ☐ Unitarian   ☐ I/we evade any reply
  ☐ Rationalist   ☐ Secularist   to a query
  ☐ Other: _____

  I/we am/are, however, an Atheist(s) and I/we hereby make application for membership in American Atheists. Both dues and contributions are to a tax-exempt organization and I/we may claim these amounts as tax deductions on my/our income tax return(s). *(This application must be dated and signed by the applicant(s) to be accepted.)*
Signature: _____ Date: _____
Signature: _____ Date: _____

  Membership in American Atheists includes a subscription to the monthly journal *American Atheist* and the monthly "Insider's Newsletter" as well as all the other rights and privileges of membership. Please indicate your choice of membership dues:

  ☐ Life, $500   ☐ Individual, $40/year
  ☐ Couple Life, $750 (Please   ☐ Age 65 or over, $20/year
      give both names above.)   (Photocopy of I.D. required.)
  ☐ Sustaining, $100/year   ☐ Unemployed, $20/year
  ☐ Couple/Family, $50/year   ☐ Student, $12/year (Photo-
      (Please give all names above.) copy of I.D. required.)

  Upon your acceptance into membership, you will receive a handsome gold-embossed membership card, a membership certificate personally signed by Dr. Madalyn O'Hair, founder of American Atheists, our special monthly "Insider's Newsletter" to keep you informed of the activities of American Atheists, and a subscription to *American Atheist*. Life members receive a specially-embossed pen and pencil set; sustaining members receive a commemorative pen. Your name will be sent to the chapter in your local area if there currently is one, and you will be contacted so you may become a part of the many local activities. Memberships and subscriptions are non-refundable.

  ☐ I/we am/are enclosing a check or money order for $_____ payable to American Atheists.
  ☐ Please charge my/our charge card for $_____ .
      ☐ Visa or ☐ Mastercard
Card #: _____
Expiration date: _____ Bank number/Code letters: _____
Signature: _____

Return form to:
American Atheists, P.O. Box 2117, Austin, TX 78768-2117